Sidecar Motorcycles

Jesse Young

Reading consultant:

John Manning, Professor of Reading

University of Minnesota

Capstone Press

MINNEAPOLIS

Printed in the United States of America.

Capstone Press • 2440 Fernbrook Lane • Minneapolis, MN 5544

Editorial Director   John Coughlan
Managing Editor   John Martin
Copy Editor   Gil Chandler

Library of Congress Cataloging-in-Publication Data

Young, Jesse, 1941-
    Sidecar motorcycles / by Jesse Young.
        p. cm.
    Includes bibliographical references and index.
    ISBN 1-56065-225-X : $13.35
    1. Motorcycle sidecars--Juvenile literature.
  [1. Motorcycle side cars]   I. Title.
  TL445.Y68   1995
  629.227'5--dc20   94-29979
                                                      CIP
                                                      AC

Table of Contents

Chapter 1

Your First Ride in a Sidecar

When you were six years old, you took your first ride in a motorcycle sidecar. You still love to take long trips in the sidecar. Now, you're on your way to the annual sidecar motorcycle races on the Isle of Man.

The Isle of Man is located in the English Channel. The TT (Tourist Trophy) Races held there are the oldest motorcycle and sidecar races in the world.

The motorcycles in the TT Races reach speeds of more than 100 miles (160 kilometers) per hour. Powerful British Norton and German BMW sidecars speed up and down the hills and through the hairpin curves.

People from all over the world come to the Isle of Man to compete. Thousands more come to watch. For the next two weeks, you will be there, too.

As the ferry docks at Douglas, the port of the Isle of Man, you realize that you're stepping onto a page of history. You may even be seeing your own future–as a sidecar racer.

You hear the sound of engines tuning to
peak performance. You rush off to watch the
sidecars and their skilled, daring riders. Right
now, there's only one place you want to be—
roadside on the Isle of Man.

BIKE

OWNER *John*

MAKE *Indian*

MODEL

Chapter 2
Early Sidecars

The first TT motorcycle and sidecar race on the Isle of Man was in 1923. But people were riding in sidecars before they were racing them. The military used them, and ordinary people enjoyed touring the countryside in their elegant sidecar motorcycles. Sidecars were practical–and very popular.

Sidecars for Work

World War I (1914-1918) helped the development of sidecars. In these light vehicles, soldiers could carry messages along the front, where the fighting often cut

Some people use sidecars for racing on ice.

telephone and telegraph lines. Sidecars were also used for carrying machine guns over rough roads. Sidecars also served as ambulances to carry the wounded.

In bombed-out areas, trailers and trucks would often get stuck in mud. But poor roads and rough ground were no problem for motor-cycles with sidecars.

After World War I, there was a huge demand for motorcycles. At that time, the economy was booming. It seemed as if the good times would last forever.

In the 1920s, sidecars appeared with screens, hoods, and hard tops. As people saw how useful sidecars were, motorcycle manufacturers began designing new and different sidecars. There was one for carrying milk churns, another to carry window-cleaning equipment, and yet another to haul the brooms used by chimney sweeps.

In 1929, the **Depression** ended the good times. All over the world, banks closed and people lost their jobs. Most motorcycle companies went out of business. In the United States, only Harley-Davidson and Indian Motorcycle survived.

Sidecars in World War II

In World War II (1939-1945), the German army used cycles with sidecars and machine guns. The BMW sidecar was a 600 cubic-centimeter (36.6 cubic-inch), **two-cylinder opposed engine**. **Driveshafts**–rather than **chain drives**–powered its rear wheels. The axle connected the BMW's rear wheel to the sidecar wheel. This allowed the bike to climb over just about anything. If necessary, German soldiers could easily disconnect the driveshaft.

With driver, **observer**, and equipment, the BMW sidecar rig weighed about a ton (590 kilograms). Still, it could travel at high speeds.

During World War II, the U.S. government ordered 500 sidecar rigs from Indian Motorcycle and Harley-Davidson. These two American companies made rugged sidecar outfits for the harsh terrain of the North African desert. But the war was nearly over when the order was completed. The companies never even delivered the sidecars.

An early sidecar motorcycle

In the years after the war, the sidecars sat in warehouses. There was little demand for motorcycles and sidecars. People were more interested in buying cars. The government sold the surplus military sidecars for almost nothing.

The modern sidecar provides nearly all the comforts of home.

Sidecar Improvements

Some minor improvements in sidecar fittings helped to keep the civilian sidecar industry alive.

Manufacturers developed more comfortable chairs with good-quality leather and thick, comfortable padding. Sports chairs–racing motorcycles fitted with sidecars–were designed to look more bullet-like.

During the 1950s and 1960s, sport sidecars continued to develop. Instead of attaching sidecars to motorcycles with bolts, companies made sidecars a part of the motorcycle **chassis** itself.

Sidecars in the 1970s

In the 1970s, sidecars became popular again. The Watsonian Company in Great Britain was swamped with orders. When Honda introduced its Gold Wing motorcycle in 1974, it became the favorite for fitting with a sidecar.

Chapter 3

Types of Sidecars

Today there are three kinds of sidecars for medium and large motorcycles.

Rigid Sidecars

The *rigid* sidecar has no suspension system and is the simplest type available. It is used mostly for racing. Because rigid sidecars have no suspension, they give bumpy rides. Many riders enjoy this.

Sprung Units

The most popular sidecars are *sprung units*. These rigs use one or more **shock-absorber**

This sprung unit has a separate suspension for the sidecar unit.

systems on the sidecar itself. Riding in a sprung unit is as comfortable as riding in a small sports car.

Flexis

The third and most sophisticated kind of sidecar is the *flexi*. This sidecar leans at the same angle as the motorcycle. Rigid and sprung units remain upright at all times. The flexi contains internal shock absorbers. It often comes with controls for handling loads of varying weights.

During a turn, the flexi leans at the same angle as the motorcycle.

Chapter 4

Owning and Driving a Sidecar

Sidecars can cost anywhere from $500 to $5,000. Most people can fit sidecars onto their bikes with simple garage tools.

Sidecars are easy to maintain. But because they weigh about 200 pounds (74.6 kilograms), they cause motorcycles to use more gas. This means it will cost you more to drive a motorcycle with a sidecar.

A sleek sidecar cuts the wind best.

This extra weight also causes the motorcycle to go about 20 miles (32 kilometers) per hour slower. With a sidecar on your motorcycle, you also have to allow for a longer braking space between vehicles.

Practical and Inexpensive

You can drive your motorcycle fitted with a sidecar in the winter, too. Because they are heavier, they maintain good traction on slippery winter roads.

Enthusiasts say sidecar motorcycles are much more economical than small family cars. Sidecar drivers also believe that a motorcycle with a sidecar causes less harm to the environment than a car. It consumes less fuel and produces less exhaust.

Driving with a Sidecar

Driving with a sidecar is definitely not the same as driving a solo motorcycle. You have to *learn* how to drive a three-wheeler. Learning how to do right-hand and left-hand turns requires practice.

Both riders have to lean into the turn as a sidecar races at high speeds.

Right turns are the hardest. When turning right, apply the front brake while opening the **throttle**. Move your body toward the sidecar to add extra weight and to keep from tipping. Using the brake and throttle this way slows the front wheel and accelerates the rear.

For the left turn, begin slowly and maintain your speed through the turn. The left turn feels much the same as on a solo motorcycle.

Brakes

If you have good brakes on your motorcycle, you won't need brakes on the sidecar. If they are poor brakes, buy a sidecar with its own brakes.

Chapter 5
Racing Sidecars

Sidecar racing is full of action. Competitors charge around the course, taking sharp turns and spectacular jumps. Motorcycles with sidecars reach speeds of more than 100 miles (160 kilometers) per hour.

Sidecars used for racing have three wheels. They use automobile wheels and **disc brakes**. Some of them also carry boat motors.

In the United States and Canada, racing engines can be no larger than 1200 cubic

centimeters (73.2 cubic inches). **Fuel injection** and **turbocharging** are against the rules.

Some companies make sidecar bodies, but most racers build their own. All sidecar rigs must conform to strict regulations.

Teamwork

Unlike other motorsports, sidecar racing takes a team of two–a driver and a passenger working together. Drivers must know how to control sidecars. They carefully control acceleration and braking through the turns. The driver also kneels over the motorcycle. This keeps the center of **gravity** lower. This way, the motorcycle doesn't topple over.

To keep all three wheels on the road, the passenger moves from one side of the sidecar to the other. He or she must stay low and use handles and toe-holds to get to the best position. The passenger often actually touches the ground. It is common to see the passenger's leather suit worn out at the elbows and shoulders from scraping the track.

A good team can keep the rig balanced even with the wheels a few inches off the ground. Their jobs demand a lot of strength and agility.

Racing Around the World

Sidecar racing has been popular in Europe and Great Britain for many years. The Grand Prix (French for "big prize") championship races take place in twelve countries. Teams earn points based on their finishes. Race winners get 20 points, for example, and the team in 15th place gets only one.

Sidecar cross teams, like motocross racers, compete over rough terrain. Like motocross, sidecar cross came to North America from Europe. It is especially popular in California.

34

Chapter 6

Sidecar Rallies

Sidecar fans hold rallies all over North America. The events at each rally may differ, but they all share the same spirit. People gather because they are enthusiastic about riding sidecar motorcycle outfits.

The Bigfoot Sidecar Club in Crater Lake, Oregon, holds a typical rally. In one of the rally events, the sidecar drivers have to drive their rigs blindfolded. The passenger shouts directions on the straights and turns.

In another event, young people ride in the sidecars. They try to throw water balloons into a bucket or to pin clothes to a clothesline. Similar games take place at rallies in Irving, Texas, and Buckhannon, West Virginia.

Chapter 7

Sidecars are Safe

Riding solo motorcycles can sometimes be dangerous. Riding a sidecar motorcycle is often less dangerous.

Adding a sidecar can make a motorcycle more stable. A motorcycle with a sidecar is also easier for other motorists to see. Sidecar motorcycles are also much less likely than solo bikes to have accidents in bad weather.

A sidecar rig will not fall over. It won't wobble on loose gravel or slide on spilled oil. In any case it is certainly safer to ride in a sidecar than behind the driver on the seat of a bike.

Chapter 8
Sidecar Popularity Today

Sidecar motorcycles continue to be popular today. Harley-Davidson still makes them, and so do European and Japanese manufacturers.

In the 1980s, two sidecar fans, Jim and Chris Dodson, could find little information about their sport. They started a magazine to provide information and increase sidecar safety awareness. Because sidecars are often called "hacks," they called the magazine *Hack'd*.

In the pages of *Hack'd,* sidecar fans can now read all about their favorite rigs and the top racers in the sport.

And there's a lot to read about–sidecars are changing all the time. There's always something new happening in the exciting world of sidecar motorcycles.

Glossary

chain drive–power is transferred from the transmission using teeth sprockets and a chain

chassis–the steel frame, attached to the axles, that holds the body and motor of the motorcycle and sidecar together

Depression–a period of unemployment and hardship during the 1930s

disc brakes–a system of braking that uses two brake pads that press against a rotating disc. Fluid pressure moves the pads.

driveshaft–a rotating shaft by which power is transferred from the transmission to the rear wheel

fuel injection–a method of injecting fuel into the combustion chamber of the engine rather than using a carburetor to supply fuel

gravity–the natural force that causes objects to move toward the center of the earth

observer–a person who rides in a sidecar

shock absorbers–hydraulic devices that absorb forces and bumps from wheels spinning over a rough surface

throttle–a lever on a motorcycle's handlebar which releases gasoline to the engine and makes the motorcycle accelerate

turbocharging–using exhaust gases to turn a turbine that forces more air-fuel mixture into the engine

two-cylinder opposed engine–two containers, sitting in opposing positions, which hold the pistons as they move up and down

To Learn More

Alth, Max. *Motorcycles and Motorcycling*. New York: Franklin Watts, 1979.

Carrick, Peter. *The Guinness Guide to Motorcycling*. London: Guinness Superlatives, 1980.

On Three Wheels: The Illustrated Encyclopedia of Motorcycles. London: Marshall Cavendish, 1979.

Some Useful Addresses

United Sidecar Association
130 South Michigan Avenue
Villa Park, IL 60181

Sidecar Racing Association
3243 Etude Drive
Mississauga, ON L4T 1S9

Hack'd: The Magazine For & About Sidecarists
P.O. Box 813
Buckhannon, WV 26201

Motorcycle Heritage Museum
33 Collegeview Road
Lesterville, OH 43081-6114

Acknowledgments

Capstone Press thanks Chris and Jim Dodson of *Hack'd: The Magazine For & About Sidecarists;* Jim and Donna Fousek; and Dan Cunningham.

Index

Photo Credits:

Sidecar Racers Association: cover, pp. 6, 7, 26, 28, 30-1; Jim and Donna Fousek: pp. 4, 14, 16, 20, 21, 22, 34, 8; Jim Dodson: pp. 8, 13; Gerry Lemmo: pp. 10, 24; Lon Kimball Studios: pp. 18-19; Cheryl Blair: p. 36.